Civil Rights Leaders

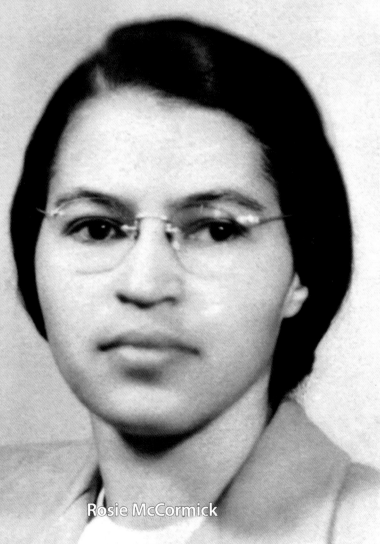

Rosie McCormick

Core Knowledge®

ISBN: 978-1-68380-490-1

Civil Rights Leaders

Table of Contents

Susan B. Anthony

Susan B. Anthony was born in Massachusetts in 1820. Her parents taught her that everyone deserves equal rights: black and white, male and female. It made her sad that in life this did not always happen.

IN THE COTTON FIELD.

One thing that made her especially sad was slavery. She wanted enslaved people to be set free. Susan also wanted all adults, not just white men, to be allowed to vote for political leaders.

When African American men were given the right to vote in 1870, Susan was pleased. But she was still unhappy that women could not vote. And why couldn't women vote? One reason was that some people at the time believed that women would vote the way their fathers or husbands told them to!

Susan decided she would vote anyway. On Election Day in November 1872, Susan and fifteen other women voted in the election for president of the United States. This was against the law, and they were arrested, but only Susan had to stand trial.

When the time came for her trial, Susan's lawyer argued that she had the right to vote because of a recent change, or amendment, to the Constitution of the United States.

The amendment said that anyone born in the country was a citizen of the United States and had all the rights of a citizen. Susan's lawyer argued that as a citizen of the United States, Susan had the right to vote.

At the trial, Susan was not allowed to speak in her own defense. The judge decided that Susan was guilty. Because she was a woman, he said, she was not allowed to vote. Then he ordered her to pay a large fine. That was her punishment.

But the judge could not stop Susan and many others from protesting and speaking out about the right of all women to vote. As the years went by, more and more people believed in this cause too.

Susan B. Anthony died in 1906, before women were allowed to vote. But her dream did not die with her. In 1920, a change to the Constitution finally gave women the right to vote.

Women voting

Susan B. Anthony

Today, we remember Susan B. Anthony. Today, women not only vote, but many become police and military officers, mayors of cities, governors of states, judges, and senators.

Barbara Jordan

Ruth Bader Ginsburg

Mary McLeod Bethune

Mary McLeod was born in 1875 in South Carolina. Her parents were freed slaves. When Mary was a little girl, she wanted to learn to read. But no one in Mary's family could teach her. There was no time for school because everyone had to work on the family farm.

Then one day a woman came to the McLeod farm and said she was starting a school for African American children. Mary wanted to go to school. Her parents agreed to let her go. Mary learned fast and taught her brothers and sisters to read.

After elementary school, Mary was given a scholarship to go to a high school for African American girls in North Carolina. At this time in the South, there was segregation. This meant that people were separated because of race. So, black children and white children did not go to the same schools. Later, Mary went to college and then returned home to teach in the school she had once gone to. Mary married and became Mary McLeod Bethune. She had a son.

Mary decided to start a school of her own for African American girls. With only $1.50 in her pocket, she moved to Daytona Beach, Florida, and did just that!

In the first year, she had only a few students. Mary collected crates and boxes for her students to sit and write on. Some people tried to scare her away, but over time more and more students came to Mary's school.

Then Mary began to teach night classes to African American men so that they could gain the skills needed to vote. During this time, only men could vote, but they had to be able to read and write.

Throughout her life, Mary believed that with an education people could improve their lives. She devoted her life to the education of African Americans.

Eleanor Roosevelt

Eleanor Roosevelt was born in 1884 in New York City. Eleanor grew up wearing beautiful clothes and lived in a fancy house with maids and servants. When she was fifteen, Eleanor was sent to a high school in England. After high school, she returned to New York.

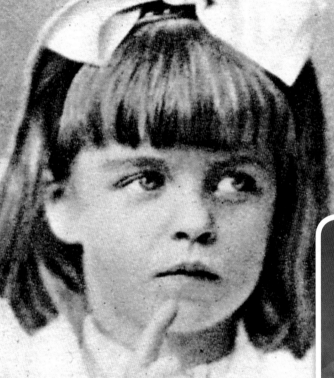

Eleanor wanted to help people who did not have as much as she did. She began to work with children who lived in poverty. It was also an exciting time for Eleanor, as her uncle, Theodore Roosevelt, had just become president of the United States.

When Eleanor was twenty-one, she married a distant cousin named Franklin Delano Roosevelt. Eleanor supported her husband as he began to work in politics. However, Franklin became sick with a disease called polio. Though in time he got better, Franklin could no longer walk easily. Eleanor helped him with his work.

When Franklin D. Roosevelt was elected president in 1932, Eleanor became the First Lady. At that time, the United States was in the middle of a difficult period called the Great Depression. Businesses failed. Some people lost their jobs and could no longer afford food.

People stood in long lines just to get something to eat. Eleanor traveled around the country to talk with those in need, visited hospitals, and served food to the poor. She told the president about the things she saw.

Mary McLeod Bethune and Eleanor Roosevelt worked together to try to help all children get a good education.

Mary McLeod Bethune and other African American leaders were invited to the White House. They wanted to help President Roosevelt and Eleanor improve the lives of African Americans, most of whom were poor.

Eleanor also felt strongly about the rights of Native Americans. She spoke out about the fact that Native Americans had lost so much of their land. As the First Lady, Eleanor had many chances to speak about the problems facing America.

Later, Eleanor Roosevelt became the first representative from the United States to the new world group called the United Nations. Mary McLeod Bethune also joined the United Nations. Eleanor and Mary helped to write a list of human rights that the UN promised to help people achieve everywhere.

Jackie Robinson

Today, baseball is a popular sport. But there was a time when African American baseball players and white baseball players did not play together. This all changed when a man named Jackie Robinson stepped out onto a baseball field in 1947. Not only was Jackie a great player, he also showed the world great courage in breaking down barriers among people.

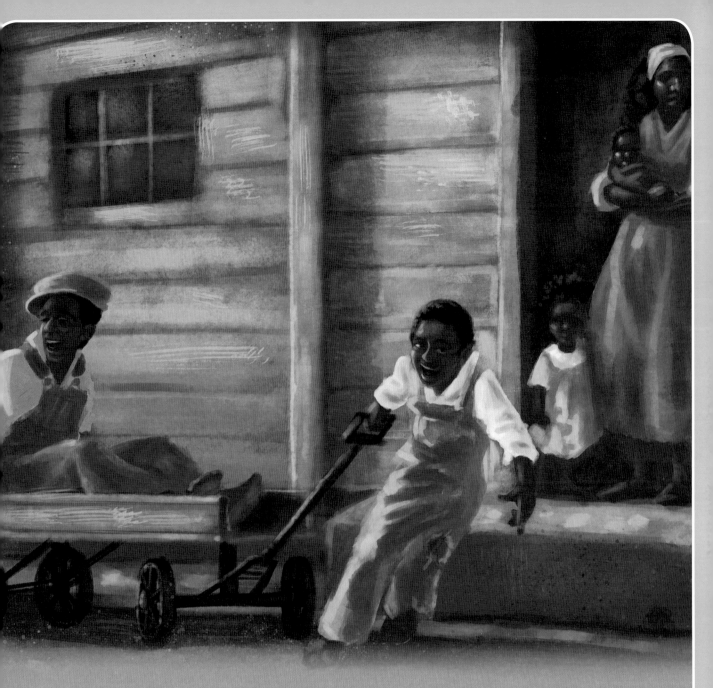

Jackie Robinson was born in 1919 in Cairo, Georgia. He was the youngest of five children. His parents were sharecroppers, people who worked the land for others for very little pay. Later, his family moved to Pasadena, California.

As a boy, Jackie was a talented athlete. In high school, he played football, basketball, baseball, and tennis, and he ran track too. After high school, Jackie went to college.

In college, Jackie competed in baseball, basketball, football, and track. He was picked for the All-American football team, which is a team of the best players from different schools around the country.

After college, Jackie began playing football for the Honolulu Bears, a Hawaiian team. When the United States entered World War II, Jackie joined the army. He became an officer.

Growing up, Jackie knew about discrimination, which was at the time legal in parts of the United States. Discrimination is the unfair treatment of people because of their skin color, race, religion, or some other reason. Jackie experienced discrimination in the army too.

When Jackie was in the army, he refused an order to sit at the back of a military bus. Jackie felt that the color of his skin should not be a reason why he could not sit where he wanted. Jackie stood trial but was found not guilty.

When Jackie left the army, he began playing baseball for the Kansas City Monarchs. The Monarchs were an all African American team.

One day, Branch Rickey, the president of the Brooklyn Dodgers, saw Jackie play. He wanted Jackie to play for the Dodgers even though they were an all-white team. Branch wanted Jackie to become the first African American to play Major League Baseball. Jackie agreed!

Jackie began playing with the Montreal Royals, a training team for the Brooklyn Dodgers. Jackie played well. Then, on April 15, 1947, Jackie Robinson put on the Brooklyn Dodgers uniform, wearing number forty-two. As the first African American player on a major league team, Jackie stepped out at Ebbets Field. Thousands of fans were there.

Jackie knew that Branch had chosen him because of his talent and his character. Jackie was strong and brave. Some players on the field—and many people in the crowd—were mean to him and called him names. But Jackie ignored them and just played baseball.

And that's what he did every time he stepped out onto the field, even when some players tried to injure him. Jackie simply played his best. In the end, he changed baseball forever. Jackie became the first African American to be included in the Baseball Hall of Fame.

Rosa Parks

Rosa Louise Parks was born in 1913 in Alabama. She grew up on a small farm with her brother, mother, and grandparents. Rosa lived during the time of legal segregation in the South. There, African Americans faced discrimination. They did not have the same rights as white people.

Because of segregation, African Americans and white people did not go to the same schools, eat at the same restaurants, or sit in the same waiting rooms. When traveling by bus, African Americans were expected to sit in certain seats, and in movie theaters they often had to sit in the balcony.

When Rosa was a little girl, she had to go to a school that was just for African American children. It was an old, one-room schoolhouse that only held classes for five months each year. Far too often there weren't enough desks or school supplies for the students. Rosa noticed that buses took white children to a new school nearby.

When Rosa was nineteen, she married Raymond Parks. Raymond was involved in the movement to improve the lives of African Americans. Rosa began to help too.

Then came the day that changed things forever. On a cold December evening in 1955, in Montgomery, Alabama, Rosa Parks left work and set off to catch the city bus that would take her home. Rosa stepped onto the bus and took a seat just behind the whites-only section.

Before long, all the seats on the bus were full, and some white people were left standing. Back then, the bus driver could tell African Americans to give up their seats to white passengers.

The bus driver did just that! He told some African American people on the bus to give up their seats. All of them did—except for Rosa. When the bus driver said he would call the police if she did not move, Rosa quietly said, "You may do that." When he asked her one more time to stand up, Rosa replied by saying, "I don't think I should have to stand up."

Before long, a police officer came. Rosa was arrested and taken to the police station. Later that night, she was released on bail.

African Americans in Montgomery who normally rode the city buses decided to show their support for Rosa by protesting. Instead of using the buses, they would walk. This kind of protest is called a boycott.

Many African American women supported the boycott, which was led by a young man named Dr. Martin Luther King Jr. The boycott lasted for 382 days. Without passengers to ride the city buses, the city couldn't afford to run the buses. Some white people supported the boycott too.

On November 13, 1956, the U.S. Supreme Court decided that it was against the law to make African Americans give up their seats. This was a great victory! Never again would an African American person have to give up their seat on a bus.

Rosa Parks's actions helped to start the civil rights movement. In fact, Rosa became known as the mother of the civil rights movement. She continued to work for civil rights her entire life.

The President of the United States of America
Awards This
Presidential Medal of Freedom
to
Rosa L. Parks

Rosa received many awards for her courage and her work. She received the Presidential Medal of Freedom in 1996 and the Congressional Gold Medal of Honor in 1999.

Martin Luther King Jr.

Martin Luther King Jr. grew up in Atlanta, Georgia, in the 1930s. As a boy growing up in the South, he too experienced unfair treatment because of the color of his skin. He experienced segregation, or being forced to use separate water fountains and restrooms.

Like his father, Martin became a church minister. He is called Dr. King because he earned a special degree called a doctorate. Martin wanted to end the unfair treatment of people of color and to replace it with legal equality.

Martin Luther King Jr. thought about Rosa Parks. The bus boycott had worked, and unfair laws were changed. He had helped with that. He had also read about another leader like himself, a man who fought injustice without using violence. That man was Mohandas (Mahatma) Gandhi, who had lived in South Africa and India.

Martin read the books Gandhi wrote and learned about the movements he had led. Gandhi said *never* to use violence when you are fighting for what is right. This reminded Martin of the Bible lesson that teaches people to walk away if someone hits them, instead of hitting back.

Martin agreed to be the leader of the civil rights movement, even though he knew he was putting himself and his family in danger. There were many people who did not like the changes he and others wanted.

Despite the dangers, Martin said that those involved in the civil rights movement must remain peaceful. He believed that a nonviolent movement that protested inequality with thoughtful words and dramatic actions—not fists and weapons—would succeed.

Martin and other ministers set about bringing together members of African American churches throughout the South. They set out to register African Americans in the South to vote. By voting, they could help bring about change.

In his first speech to the leaders of African American churches in the South, Martin said:

We have no alternative but to protest. For many years we have shown an amazing patience. We have sometimes given our white brothers the feeling that we liked the way we were being treated. But we come here tonight to be saved from that patience that makes us patient with anything less than freedom and justice.

And so it began. African Americans living in Southern states began to hold sit-ins at lunch counters that would not serve them. Sit-ins were nonviolent protests that involved people sitting down in places where they were often not allowed.

People rode buses from state to state and protested in places that allowed segregation. They marched in the streets.

Many people were arrested for taking part in these peaceful protests. Martin was arrested many times.

Then, in 1963, Martin led a march on Washington, D.C. Thousands of people came to Washington to hear people speak in front of the Lincoln Memorial.

Martin gave his famous "I Have a Dream" speech. In this speech, he said that he hoped for a day when people would be judged not by the color of their skin, "but by the content of their character."

The following year, Martin was given one of the highest awards anyone can achieve: the Nobel Peace Prize.

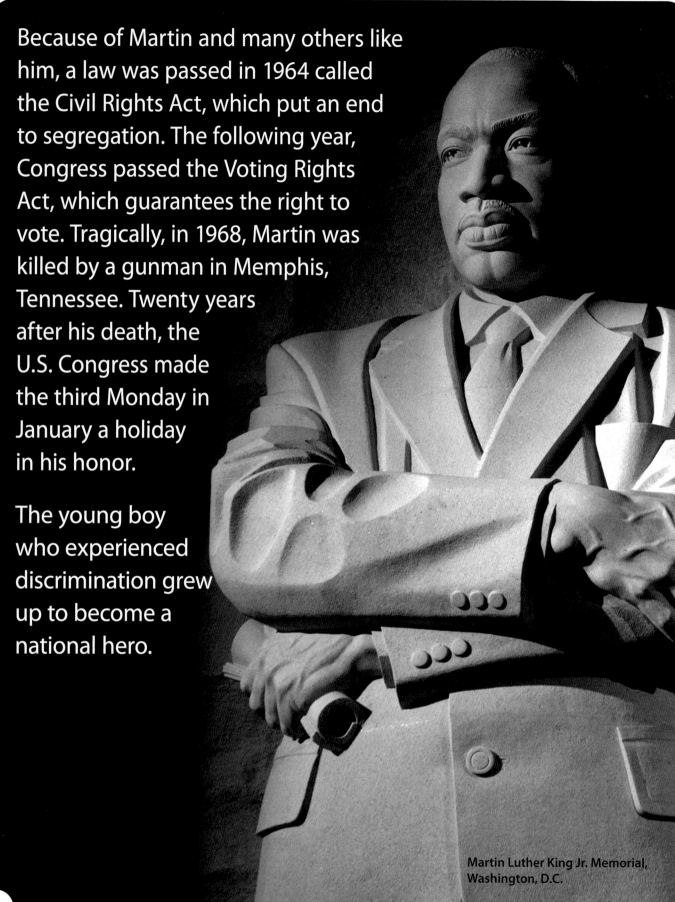

Because of Martin and many others like him, a law was passed in 1964 called the Civil Rights Act, which put an end to segregation. The following year, Congress passed the Voting Rights Act, which guarantees the right to vote. Tragically, in 1968, Martin was killed by a gunman in Memphis, Tennessee. Twenty years after his death, the U.S. Congress made the third Monday in January a holiday in his honor.

The young boy who experienced discrimination grew up to become a national hero.

Martin Luther King Jr. Memorial, Washington, D.C.

Cesar Chavez

Cesar Chavez was born in Arizona in 1927. His parents were farmers. When he was ten years old, his family moved to California to become migrant farmworkers. Migrant farmworkers work on someone else's farm, picking the ripe fruits and vegetables. Then they move on. They migrate, or move, from farm to farm.

At each farm, Cesar's family would live in a small, crowded home. As soon as the crops were picked, the family migrated to the next farm. Cesar's family moved around so much that, as a child, he went to more than thirty different elementary schools. When he finished the eighth grade, Cesar left school to work on farms full time.

A few years later, Cesar joined the U.S. Navy. He was a soldier in World War II. After the war, he returned to California and worked on farms. But Cesar wanted to make life better for migrant farmworkers.

Cesar became a leader. He knew that migrant workers worked very hard for very little pay. He also knew they had very few rights. So, Cesar began to meet with farmworkers and farm owners about better pay and working conditions.

When the farm owners refused to listen, Cesar and his friend, Dolores Huerta, led a strike. The strike meant that, as a protest, the farmworkers stopped working in the fields. They led protest marches too!

The farm owners still would not listen. And so, as time went by, the fruits and vegetables rotted in the fields. The workers became scared. While they were on strike, they couldn't earn the money they needed to support their families.

Cesar kept their courage up. He decided to ask other Americans for help. Cesar asked people all across the country to boycott, or stop buying, crops such as grapes that were grown on the farms where migrant workers worked. He told people about how hard life was for migrant workers.

Many Americans listened to Cesar and stopped buying grapes and other things to show the farm owners they agreed with the workers on strike.

The strike went on for a long time. Then Cesar decided to go a hunger strike—he did not eat for twenty-five days!

This got the attention of the whole country. People learned about the farmworkers' problems. Finally, after five years, the farm owners agreed to pay the farmworkers more money and to make their jobs and houses better. Cesar ended his hunger strike by sharing bread with Senator Robert F. Kennedy. He had succeeded!

Extraordinary People

History books are filled with the names of people who have stood up against injustice. In this book, we have highlighted just seven people who worked to create a fairer and more equal American society. But of course there are others. Here's a short glimpse at the achievements of five more extraordinary people who have made a difference.

Chief Standing Bear was the leader of the Ponca, a Native American nation that lived in Nebraska. The Ponca's land was taken away by the American government. Standing Bear brought a lawsuit against the U.S. Army for removing his people from their land. Standing Bear won the lawsuit, and the Ponca returned to Nebraska. Standing Bear was the first Native American to speak before a federal court. Today, there is a statue of him in the U.S. Capitol.

Three African American women were once described as "human computers" because of their brilliant minds. But perhaps what is even more impressive is the fact that all three women had successful careers as mathematicians and engineers during a time when black people faced discrimination and segregation. Despite being treated unfairly, these women worked on the early American space program.

Dorothy Vaughan grew up to become a mathematician and a computer programmer. Dorothy went to work for NASA, where she became a leading computer expert.

Katherine Johnson was a mathematician who worked on U.S. space programs that sent astronauts to the moon.

Mary Jackson was also a mathematician and engineer. Mary became NASA's first black female engineer.

Juan Felipe Herrera was born in California in 1948. He is the son of migrant farmers who worked on farms picking crops. As a boy, Juan had to move a lot because his family had to go wherever there was work. After graduating high school, Juan went to college. Juan became a famous writer. He is a poet and the author of many children's books. But Juan has never forgotten how difficult life is for migrant workers.

Core Knowledge®

CKHG™

Core Knowledge HISTORY AND GEOGRAPHY™

Editorial Directors

Linda Bevilacqua and Rosie McCormick

Subject Matter Expert

Spencer A. Leonard, PhD

Consultant

Gerald L. Terrell, Sr.

Illustration and Photo Credits